CASINO GAMBLING
FOR
WINNERS!

Moe Shuckelman

GOLLEHON BOOKS™
GRAND RAPIDS, MICHIGAN

Library of Congress Catalog Card Number: 96-94005

ISBN 0-914839-50-0
(International Standard Book Number)

GOLLEHON is an exclusive trademark of Gollehon Press, Inc.

GOLLEHON BOOKS are published by: Gollehon Press, Inc.,
6157 28th St. SE, Grand Rapids, MI 49546.

GOLLEHON BOOKS are available in quantity purchases;
contact Special Sales. Gollehon does not accept unsolicited
manuscripts. Brief book proposals are reviewed.

Contents

Important
Legal Disclaimer

Other books authored
by Moe Shuckelman

How To Get Laid In Las Vegas
Without Even Trying

How To Lose Money Buying Stocks
On The Internet

Brain Surgery For The Novice

All About Farm Animals

How To Cheat At Golf

Most of the answers in this book
should not be taken seriously.
Casino Gambling For Winners is a parody
of the literally hundreds of gambling books
on the market.
It is intended to let you stop and look back
at what gambling should really be.

Fun.

*To gamblers who still have
their sense of humor*

Chapter One

Stuff

How To Tell
If You're A Loser...

Only a real loser will notice that the pictures on the cover of this book all represent a typically losing situation. Look at the blackjack hand. Do you see this often? If you do, you're a loser. It's the worst hand you can get! When you throw dice, do you get one lousy dot on each face staring you in the kisser? That's a craps; it's a loser, like you are. And what about those green numbers on the roulette wheel? Do you never bet them and they hit, then start betting them and they don't? Yep, you're a loser.

Oh, about that video poker hand… garbage, right? Well, it's a straight, and it's a *winning* hand. But it doesn't look like much to a loser, does it? Guess how many times a hand like this gets thrown away!

You see, casinos are built on losers. That's why if you're a loser, you really shouldn't read this book. The casinos need losers so they can put in some new marble floors, a few more chandeliers, a bigger pool, add another thousand rooms, you know, important stuff like that.

Just think, if it weren't for players like you, these places wouldn't even exist!

Attention
Slow Readers...

Here's your chance to actually read a book cover to cover. It's only 150 pages... a piece of cake! You'll be dashing through this "volume" in no time. And what's more, you can tell all your friends you just finished a great book. That's right. *Finished!* You will have actually read an *entire* book!

Remember all those great tomes you were supposed to read in high school? "Uh, well, teacher, my pet alligator ate the library's only copy of *War And Peace* before I had a chance to even open the cover. I think he ate it 'cause I spilled ketchup on it."

Buy this book for your own peace of mind. No more insidious fears that you're so stupid you can't even read a simple book. No more inferiority complexes. No sir! You are about to read an entire, full-length, feature book!

And listen… if you can't read, buy it anyhow for the pictures.

Or try a little ketchup.

Attention Readers Who Are Into Weird Stuff...

A few people who have read this book claim that it has hidden messages. That's right. There are hidden secrets to be found in the very book you are holding, but you have to read the book backward to get them. The messages come from the god, Yo, who is responsible for every eleven that has ever been rolled on a dice table. Boy, how nice it would be to get connected to this guy. Here's a tip: If you have trouble reading backward, order the Chinese edition.

From The Publisher...

An Open Letter To The IRS

We understand that author Moe Shuckelman is being audited. He first told us that he had won untold thousands of dollars at the blackjack tables, and tens of thousands of dollars betting football. We figured he'd say anything to get his book published.

Now he says it's all a big lie. He's broke! The last football game he claims he actually won was the Baltimore Colts over the St. Louis Cardinals.

He also wants us to announce that he has sold everything and moved to Guam.

Chapter Two

Q's & A's

What if I find a spot open at a blackjack table but there's no room to get my chair in?

Yeah, this happens because the casinos like to squeeze in seven spots on a table that comfortably seats only six players.

But, if you really want to play at such a crowded table, I suppose you can always lean over a player, spill his drink, knock over his chips, screw up the cards, lose the bet, and walk away with everyone thinking you're the biggest idiot in the world.

The last time I gambled, the casino picked up all my food and gave me a nice suite. They really take good care of me. Trouble is, I lost ten grand at the tables. Any advice?

It seems to me that it is you who is taking good care of the casino!

My advice is stop playing for comps, and start playing to win!

I see these guys just hanging around behind the tables... I think they're called pit bosses, or something. What exactly do these guys do, anyhow?

They have four basic responsibilities:

1. Keep out cheaters, criminals, hookers, card-counters, lawyers, and other "undesirables."

2. Prepare markers and authorize chips for credit players. As a rule, the bosses are slow with the chips when the table's hot, and fast with the chips when the table's cold.

3. Watch the dealers, particularly the female dealers. Sometimes this important duty is also extended to cocktail waitresses.

4. Stand around. Most pits have at least two bosses so there's always someone to lean against.

It really bothers me the way some people gamble. And not just blackjack players. There are times I want to just scream out, "Don't hit that!"

I think I'm going to start helping players who don't

know what they're doing. I assume you do that all the time, right?

Wrong! I keep my mouth shut unless someone asks for advice. And even then I'm hesitant to offer *specific* advice.

Two things come to mind with your observation: One, if you offer to help—tell a player to hit or stand, for example— it's guaranteed the hand will lose. I absolutely guarantee you will make a fool of yourself. And speaking of fools, there's an old adage I particularly like about dispensing advice:

Wise men don't need it, and fools won't heed it.

I know a guy who goes to casinos just to play keno. Can you believe it? Keno?!

Sure. A friend of mine has concocted this weird ticket that costs $72 to play, but he's got something like 144 ways to win. Basically, he makes his bet, waits an hour for the numbers to come up, then goes up and bets it again. Waits another hour, and then bets it again. I mean… it goes on and on like this!!

Never bet $72 of your hard-earned money on this stupid game. Even if you've got plenty of money, don't waste it on a keno ticket because—I'm telling you—it won't hit! And I don't

care how you make your
money. Even the dirtiest,
filthiest drug money is too
good for this game!

**All the blackjack experts tell
me I should never take
insurance when the dealer
has an ace up. Is that true?**

Yes. Never take insurance
unless you're flying home on
Acme Airlines.

I take four-day gambling trips about twice a year. When I get to the casino, I'm so anxious to hit the tables and then I play for so long that I'm wiped out the first day.

What should I do the next time I go?

Here's a case where the answer lies in your planning. It's obvious that the first day of your four-day trips is the real problem here, so simply skip the first day and take three-day trips.

Are some dice tables better than others?

Yes. And those are always the tables that you're not at, and can't get to because they're too crowded. But when you do get there, the table turns cold, and the table you left instantly gets hot.

♥ ♥ ♥ ♥

I'm an old-timer who likes to go to the racetrack and bet the ponies. But I don't do very well. Any tips?

First, you have to find out which races are fixed.

I was watching a game I bet on TV and all this jerk at the free-throw line had to do was make one lousy free-throw and I win. He missed 'em both. Can you believe it? This bum cost me a hundred bucks!

Do you realize that all the bettors who had the other side won because of the same reason you lost? They had to share the same anxiety that you did, thinking the shooter could not possibly miss two out of two.

But more importantly, my guess is you're not only an expert at picking losers, but an absolute genius at picking someone else to blame.

♣ ♣ ♣ ♣

The other day I put a quarter in this video poker machine, and it kept dropping through to the coin tray. Can you check this out for me?

Yeah, I checked it out. You can't put quarters in a dollar machine. But don't feel stupid. I did this once, too. I put quarters in what looked like a quarter machine and it wouldn't take them, either. It said 25 cents right there on the machine! But on closer look, it didn't say 25 cents, it said

25 *dollars!* This fancy machine took twenty-five-dollar tokens! No wonder nobody was playing them!

◆ ◆ ◆ ◆

When I play blackjack, I always get 16s, 15s, and 14s. I never get 20s. The dealer gets all the 20s. I just lost my job, my dog bit me, my wife left me, and my kid wrecked my car last week. What can I do to change my luck?

I think you have me confused with Ann Landers.

What can I do if I want to play dice at a hot table where the shooter's been going after the same point for 15 minutes... but there's no room?!

Just go ahead and cram yourself in. And let me tell you exactly what will happen next because I know you... every dice player knows you.

You'll light a cigarette with a Zippo that throws a three-foot flame. The players beside you will check to make sure their hair's not on fire. Then, you'll stop the game by betting all the numbers at once with a bunch of wadded-up bills that takes an eon to count. The time this will take is directly proportional to the time it takes for you to create a one-inch ash on the end of your cigarette that's constantly moving up and down because it's stuck to your lips. As you mumble something stupid like, "Let's get this game going," you'll drop your ash on the table just as the dice are about to finally start flying again. You'll reach down to brush it away and… bingo! You'll say something stupid like, "Boy, those dice sure have sharp corners on 'em!" The stickman will say, "Seven-out." And what the other players will say I can't print here, but you'll want to keep your Zippo handy just to protect yourself.

Please explain the term "past-posting." Isn't this a term used at a racetrack?

It's a term associated with all kinds of gambling. It simply refers to the act of making a wager, or increasing it, *after* you already know the bet won. If you want to learn exactly how to do this, pick up a copy of Morris Chelman's book, *Everything You Should Have Known About Cheating Before You Got Caught.* You can write to Morris in care of The Big House, Leavenworth, Kansas.

My friend tells me that blackjack is the most popular table game in the casino. Why?

Probably because so many "experts" preach that the game has such a modest percentage for the house, on the order of one percent or less. Some even make unqualified claims that the percentage can actually favor the player.

What they fail to tell you is that such low percentages only apply to the most astute players who play each hand flawlessly under optimum playing conditions. They also fail to mention that even such low percentages will eventually knock out all but the hardiest of players. Plus, they fail to tell you that the percentages only swing to the player's favor a rare portion of the time, with most players not being able to discern the difference.

For the great majority of players—those who know only a little about the game—the percentages are at least four or five percent against them. Not much better than hanging around the roulette wheel. And not much of a funny answer, either. But I wanted you to know that.

When I give dealers a tip, why do they always tap the chip on the table before putting it in their shirt pocket?

Tapping the chip on the table indicates to the floorman watching the game that it's indeed a tip. The floorman always watches the dealers to be sure they don't steal. A pit boss watches all the floormen to be sure *they* don't steal. A shift boss watches all the pit bosses to be sure *they* don't steal. A casino manager watches all the shift bosses to be sure *they* don't steal. The casino owner watches the casino manager to be sure *he* doesn't steal. The IRS watches the casino owner to be sure *he* doesn't steal. And that's where it ends because we all know we can trust the IRS.

My wife and I like to play roulette. We were married in 1938 so we like to play number 38. But—can you believe it?—all the times we've played it, it's never come up.

Of course not, you bonehead! There's no 38 on the wheel! It stops at 36. There's 38 spots, but that's only because there's also a single zero and a double zero. You're a triple zero!!

I swear every time the dice go off the table the shooter rolls a loser-seven. What do you think about this?

If you'd stop swearing every time the dice go off the table, maybe you wouldn't lose.

Do you realize your swearing is causing all the other players to lose, too?

I think the gods of Chance have had all they're going to take of you, buddy.

Some guy told me you're better off just betting college football, and staying away from the pros. Is he right?

Right on the money! The pros are much less predictable. But regardless of which teams you bet, there's a bigger problem here.

Unless you live in Nevada, do you really want to do business with Fat Tony? Do you know what it's like trying to collect from this guy?

"You wanted da Dolphins?! I taut ya said da Colts!! *You* owe me two big ones. I don't owe *you* nuttin'!"

Is there any relationship between the time of day and your chances of winning? I always seem to do better in the late afternoon.

Well, I suppose you stand a good chance of *not* losing during the late evening hours and the wee hours of the morning. That's assuming you're up in your room sleeping.

I always recommend that players sleep a lot during a gambling trip. Remember my advice:

If you don't snooze, you lose.

At the dice tables, I've heard it said that you can always identify good shooters by the way they look, and the way they play.
  Is this right?

Wrong! The last good shoot I saw came from an old lady who told me afterward why she did so well:
  "You have to know how to flip those, uh, um, those...uh, you know... red balls with corners on them."

Hazel and I are just a couple of old ladies who like to go to the casino and play the poker machines. But we can only afford to play one quarter at a time. Our friends say we should always play five quarters at a time. Who's right?

Your friends are giving you good advice because if you hit the big royal, you'll get a bigger than linear payoff with five coins invested.

In other words, two coins pay two times the winnings for one coin, three coins pay three times the winnings for one coin, etc. But five coins pay more than five times the winnings for one coin. In the case of a progressive jackpot, it might be 20 times as much. The old adage holds true: Don't build up a jackpot you're not trying to win.

Surprisingly, this is the very first case on record where "a friend" actually gave good advice. Usually, "a friend" will tell you to only play the machines by the door, or at the end of a row, or a machine that feels warm, or that doles out warm coins, or a machine that was recommended by the change girl (my favorite), or that is overdue (there is no such thing), or *don't* play a machine that has just emptied (actually a better reason *to* play it).

I want to try my luck at being a professional blackjack player. Can I get into this elite group?

Yeah. You're a shoe-in.
Get it?

When I play craps, it seems as if the table's cold most of the time. Is there any way to tell when I walk up?

A craps table *is* cold most of the time! You wouldn't expect it to be hot most of the time, would you? Otherwise, we could all play craps for a living.

But to answer your question, yes, you can get an idea how a

table's doing when you walk up by checking out the other players. See if you can sense their mood.

If most players seem a little grouchy, pass it up. Trouble is, most dice players are a little grouchy anyhow, so it's not the best test.

Better yet, note how many chips they have in front of them. If the players are grasping a small handful of chips, or if there are few chips in the racks in front of them, my guess is they've now progressed beyond "grouchy" to "really pissed."

Move on.

My wife and I like to play slots, but I've got this little problem, you see. When I carry rolls of quarters in my pockets, I'm afraid I can't hold my pants up. The wife says I've got the classic "pear" shape, you know what I mean?

You aren't the same guy I saw working under my kitchen sink last month, are you? Just kidding. Listen, I've got great news for you. Most all casinos are going to coin-less slots, if they haven't already.

Many slot machines today have a built-in bill changer but even that's old technology. Look for the new machines that will allow you to insert your slot-club card and simply play "on account." You'll deposit a certain amount of money when you arrive, or you might be able to play on credit, just like writing a marker at the table games.

So go ahead, drink all the beer you like!

I just sent in $500 for a blackjack system that guarantees I'll be a big winner. I've included a copy of the ad so you can look it over. Do you think it was worth it?

Are you kidding?!
This system you bought is incredible! It's the only one out there that really works! Even boneheads can win with it! I've heard stories of people with only a grade-school education who bought it and now live in big mansions with a Mercedes in both garages.

You're on your way to riches, buddy. By the way, as soon as

your check clears, I'll put the stuff in the mail.

If a train from Albuquerque is traveling to Vegas at an average speed of 53 miles per hour and has one derailment, and another train leaves the station 55 minutes later but travels at an average speed of 59 miles per hour with two derailments, which one gets there first?

Do you have an airport?

I have bad credit. Can I get any credit in a casino?

Sure. But only if you use someone else's name. Don't use mine!

How do casinos check a guy's credit?

They go back, way back, to the day you bought your very first car. Oh, and remember that dentist you stiffed for fifty bucks? Now he's going to come back and haunt you.

What if I get credit, use it all up, and then can't pay it back?

You have three options here. One, you can call the credit manager and set up a payment plan. Two, you can move to Canada. Three, remember that dentist you stiffed for fifty bucks?

Where I play blackjack, we don't have any single-deck or double-deck games. Counting seems to be a waste of time and I can't find any excitement in the game anymore. What can I do to restore my interest in this game?

You're right, there's not much excitement in the game without the challenge of counting. So why not look at some other games?

I play only craps now, and find that the excitement and anxiety of the game are what pulled me away from the blackjack tables. In fact, I'll never again play blackjack against a 6- or 8-deck shoe.

Here's a list of things I'd rather do:

1. Watch reruns of "Full House."

2. Eat Brussels sprouts (without cheese sauce).

3. Do my Christmas shopping.

4. Pet my neighbor's Rottweiler.

5. Take my Buick in for service.

6. Go to the dentist.

7. Listen to "Achy Breaky Heart."

8. Get a rectal exam.

9. Stand in line at Disneyland.

10. Eat airplane food.

I'm a hockey player and just got a new goalie mask for my birthday. I thought this might make a good disguise since I'm also a known card-counter. Any problem wearing my mask while I'm playing blackjack?

Do it only on Halloween. On second thought, go ahead and try it anytime. My guess is the pit bosses will leave you alone.

♣ ♣ ♣ ♣

I just read about some guy who hit a casino for over $2 million at the baccarat tables. What I want to know is who is this guy, where did he do it, and how?!

I think it was Col. Mustard, in the library, with a candlestick.

Here's the way I play craps... I buy the 4 and 10 for a quarter, place the 5 and 9 for fifty, the 6 and 8 for sixty, cover all the hardways for a hundred, and any craps for a quarter. What do you think?

That's not the way you play. That's the way you lose! Obviously, you like to "jump in" don't you? Let me ask you a personal question: When you draw your bath water, don't you stick your big toe in first to "test the waters"?

The question is more relevant than you think. In years gone by, dice tables were called tub tables, because they were shaped like tubs. For you... appropriate.

When I bet football, I never bet the Lions. Anything wrong with that?

Makes perfectly good sense to me. I always say you should stay away from teams that beat you time and time again. Of course, I'm sure you also know that when you *don't* bet them, they cover.

When I've found a good table, I yell for my wife to come over. Something like, "Hey, Mildred, get over here!" But a friend of mine says that's not a good idea. Why not?

Never, under any circumstances, summon your wife to the table. Most wives can "frost" a table within ten yards.

My friend uses what he calls a "betting progression" at all the table-games. He claims it works.

What exactly *is* a betting progression and is there any long-term value to it?

It's a "system" of changing the size of your bet based on some stupid formula like 1-2-2-4-4-2. Your first bet is one chip, your second is two chips, and so on. When you complete the progression you start over again.

Here's what you need to know about systems:

They only make money for the casino and the guy who sells them.

I'm tired of blackjack. Now I'm thinking about playing craps instead, but it looks complicated.
   Do you recommend this?

   Not surprisingly, there are a lot of disenchanted blackjack players out there who have migrated to the dice tables. In fact, craps is fast becoming the casino's most popular table-game. It's *less* complicated than blackjack if you follow the basic game.
   Craps is definitely the most fun of the two. But definitely the most risky.
   "Hey, what happened to all my chips?!"

I read in a book once that the payback on some video poker machines is actually greater than 100 percent. How could this be?

Most video poker machines are from 92 to 99 percent, with the majority of Nevada machines around 97 percent. The percentages are based on the paytables that the machine proudly displays for you on the feature-glass or on the actual screen.

But, on some progressives, it's possible the royal-flush jackpot could reach such a high amount that the percentages roll over to the player's favor.

Now don't get too excited about it because it's only based on the inflated value of the royal, not all the other payouts for smaller hits. In other words, the player's "edge" is buried in the big jackpot, and you have to hit it to realize it.

The "realization" comes when a smiling attendant is counting out hundred-dollar bills in your hand! Maybe *both* hands!

Maybe the jackpot is so big the casino wants to give you a check! Wow! Yes! More! More! Give me more!!

But like I said, don't get too excited about it.

If I win a lot of money, I'm worried about carrying it around with me or leaving it in my room. Where's the best place to hide it?

Take it up to your room, put it in a plastic baggie, and hide it in the toilet bowl. Be sure to drop the lid.

You gotta know that no one in their right mind would ever look in there. But for gosh sakes, don't flush it!

I just moved to Las Vegas. Last night I lost $500 playing blackjack. The night before, I lost over a thousand. Last week I lost the rent money. I'm going to give it another shot tomorrow to see if I can win it all back. For now, I'm living out of my car. Any suggestions?

I think you might want to consider living in Pleasantville, Ohio. As of this writing, it is the only city in America that does not even have an Indian casino nearby. You should be safe there. In fact, I'd gas up right now while you still have your car.

A blackjack dealer got mad at me once for blowing a little cigarette smoke in her face. What does she expect in a casino? I have a right to smoke, don't I?

Yes. There's nothing wrong with smoking at a blackjack table, as long as you don't exhale.

I'm a blackjack dealer who's fed up with all the crazies I get at my table. I've had players call me terrible names when I beat them. But I'm just a dealer. I'm not trying to beat anybody. I just deal the cards. One guy called me a "bitch." Another guy tried to grab my boobs. And once, this jerk kept blowing his cigarette smoke in my face… on purpose! How can I get away from people like this?

I know a guy who's just about ready to leave for Pleasantville, Ohio. I'm sure he's got room for you. If you hurry, you can still catch him.

I've been told casinos have these big vaults hidden somewhere in the back. What's in these big vaults anyhow?

Geraldo Rivera.

♣ ♣ ♣ ♣

I'm 89 years old and love to play craps. I have trouble standing, but I can always stand at a dice table. I live in Vegas now and go to the same casino just about every day. Everybody knows me there. I'm gonna level with you... I'm worried that my time is running out. There's probably not much you can

do for me, but I just wanted to write.

Well, there's a couple of things. For one, stay away from Jack Kevorkian. For another, I think you've got nothing to worry about. You see, I've always believed that when I buy the farm (probably by betting it), there will still be some good action left up there.

Yes, it is my firm conviction that there are dice tables in heaven. But what really worries me is the other place. That's probably where all the hot tables are!

Oh, you don't think hell has dice tables? Where else do you think all the pit bosses go?

Should I always double down on 10 or 11 when the dealer has a little card showing?

Yes. Here's the way it works: When you double down, you'll get a little crummy card, the dealer will not bust, and you'll lose your bet. When you *don't* double down when you should, you'll get a *good* card, or the dealer will bust.

It never fails.

♥ ♥ ♥ ♥

When should I make my biggest bets?

When you're drunk.

What happens if I'm caught cheating in Vegas?

In the old days, the casino owners would have you taken out in the desert and let you sun-bathe for a very long time. Today, of course, they don't do that. They only break your knees.

Should I be polite to the dealers and call them "Sir" or "Ma'am" and say "Thank you" when I win?

Not unless you're Beaver Cleaver.

Can I quit my job and become a professional blackjack player?

Yes, you can do that. You can win big money playing just an hour or two each day. And if you believe that, give me a call. I've got a great deal on some land down in Florida that I can let you in on, cheap.

Is there a particular rule for splitting face cards?

Yes! Only split face cards if you're a moron. (Ever notice how many morons there are at the blackjack tables?)

I've heard of blackjack
players who use a
sophisticated computer
strapped inside their shorts
with wires running down to
little buttons under their
toes so they can secretly
keep track of the values of
cards they see.

The computer tells them
when to hit or stand by
giving off a little tingle in
their shorts.

Does this thing work?

With batteries, yes. But never
plug the contraption into a wall
socket!

I have a problem with my husband. When we're ready to quit playing slots, he says, "One more roll." So he goes and gets another roll of quarters.

Do you know how many times he gets "one more roll"? About ten times, that's how many!

What can I do to make him stop this?

Casinos thrive on the notion of "One Mo' Time!"

And it isn't just rolls of coins. It can be "one more shoe," or "one more marker," or "one more shooter."

Here's the solution for you:

Carry a small hammer in your purse. A 16-oz. claw-hammer works best. The next time your husband goes back for the second "one more roll" of quarters, simply hit him over the head with it. Just be sure you don't hit him with the "claw" end, unless you have other problems you didn't tell me about.

♥ ♥ ♥ ♥

What can I do to beat these one-arm bandits?

Learn how to make your own slugs.

I've read all the really good blackjack books, and I've read yours, too. I think I'm finally ready to become a professional player, but my wife's trying to talk me out of it. What are my chances?

The term *professional* generally means you're so good at something that you can make a living at it. The last professional blackjack counter I met lived in a run-down trailer park and had to get rides to the casinos because his rusted-out '89 Chevy didn't run. It didn't run because he couldn't afford to get it fixed. I suppose you could say he eked out a living, but get real, buddy. Throw out all the "really good" blackjack books before your wife throws *you* out!

♣ ♣ ♣ ♣

I have a bad habit of counting and recounting my chips while I'm playing. It's just a nervous habit but sometimes it affects my concentration on the game. How do I stop this?

It really isn't necessary to count all your chips while you're playing. Wait until you're finished and then you won't have to bother.

There's this guy I've ran into at the dice tables who always carries a duck call with him. Keeps it right there with his chips. Whenever he has a bet on a hard 4, and it hits, he blows the damn thing as loud as he can. What gives?

He's having fun. Something that too few players really understand anymore. You are there to enjoy yourself and to enjoy the chance of winning.

A pair of 2s, incidentally, is a pair of ducks to old-time dice players.

Hi, my name is Lance. I'm a card-counter and I know the importance of wearing a disguise when I play blackjack. I play so much, and play so well, that most pit bosses used to recognize me and throw me out. But now I wear women's clothes—a wig, make-up, the whole nine yards. No one suspects me. The problem is, when I get home I kind of like to keep the outfit on.

You don't need a disguise. You need an operation.

I like to tip the dealers, but sometimes they don't deserve a tip. Is there any set of guidelines for tipping in a casino?

Well, I have my own list that I'm happy to share with you.

Do not tip a dealer who:

1. Flips all the cards in your face.

2. Offers to sell you a fake Rolex.

3. Tells you he needs money for his sick kids.

4. Complains that you woke him up.

5. Tries to look up your nose.

6. Wears a button that says, "I break for lawyers."

7. Taps his fingers when it's your turn to play.

8. Refuses to tie your shoes for you.

9. Says he just got tested and he's clean.

How can I find out the percentages on a reel-type slot machine?

It's a rather secret equation, and it does require a little bit of math, but I'll share it with you: $E=MC^2$. "M" is the number of reels on the machine, and "C" has something to do with the speed of light.

What should I do after I just won thousands of dollars at the dice tables?

Feel guilty taking the poor casino's hard-earned money.

♠ ♠ ♠ ♠

Should I offer to give some of it back?

No need. You probably will anyhow.

♥ ♥ ♥ ♥

I want to write to you about the way some of these girls dress who deal cards. See-through blouses, low-cut blouses... I think it's a

shame that some casinos would stoop to this level.

Yeah, and you know what? Some players will "accidentally" drop a card just to make the dealer stoop to that level you're talking about.

Anyhow, the only thing I could find on this is casino regulation 6B which requires female blackjack dealers to have no more than one blouse button open while dealing. If you find a female dealer with two or more buttons unbuttoned, report this serious infraction to any pit boss immediately. The pit boss will look into it!

I like the live table games and can't understand why anyone would want to play blackjack or keno, for example, on a machine! Even plain slots seem too impersonal to me. Am I right?

Well, there's no right or wrong answer.

Some people like the social atmosphere of dice tables or blackjack tables while others like the more intimate one-on-one "relationship" with a machine.

Casino executives, with an eye to the future, suggest that sometime all blackjack games will be dealt by machines.

I'm sure you know that machines are used today to shuffle the cards... so why not deal them, too?

The technology exists for automated dice games and even roulette tables. The machines are coming whether you like them or not.

Indeed, machines are going to play a big role in the casino of the future. But pit bosses are here to stay.

No self-respecting machine would ever be caught dead playing the role of a pit boss!

I'm curious. What's the total value of all the chips in the dealer's chip-tray?

That's something you'll never have to worry about.

What happens if the dealer runs out of chips in the tray?

That's something you'll never have to worry about.

What happens if I try to steal some chips out of the dealer's chip-tray?

That's something you'll have a lot of time to worry about.

Is there any way to defeat the casino's security system and rip them off?

Yes. Trace the phone lines from the main telephone pole in front of the casino. The lines are usually strung to the back of the casino. Cut these wires.

Then, walk through the door marked "Employees Only" with your wheel-barrow (used to haul out all the cash). If you act cool, no one will notice.

Incidentally, the room you're looking for says "Count Room" on the door. Knock three times (the casino's secret code) and tell the guy you're filling in for the regular guy who's sick.

Remember, act cool.

Isn't blackjack an easy game to play?

No. All the different rules and player options make the game complicated.

Since most players aren't skilled, they lose. They make a bet, the dealer takes it away; they make another bet, the dealer takes it away.

Wait a minute. Maybe this game *is* easy!

During the first three or four weeks of pro football, I like to just practice making my picks. Sort of like getting in shape, you know? I can't miss when I'm just picking for fun. But later when I actually bet my picks, most of them lose. What's going on? Is it just psychological?

Yeah. It's like my golf game. When I'm on the practice tees, I'm dynamite. And when I'm on the course, my practice swings are absolutely flawless. So why am I carrying a 30 handicap?!

I live in the East but I like to gamble in Vegas. It's great out there, man! I mean, Atlantic City is OK, but there's no place like Vegas, you know what I mean? But I can't stand those five-hour flights. There's got to be a faster way to get there, man. And, hey, Mr. S., I got all your books. I love you, man!

Well, since we don't have "transporter" technology yet, I really don't know of any faster way to get to Vegas than a jet. I mean, you just can't beam yourself out there... know what I mean? So here's a suggestion:

For your next trip, ask your travel agent to book you on a wide-open flight during a time the airlines call "off peak."

Once you get up in the air, look for a whole row of seats that are open. Go get a couple of pillows and a blanket, lift up the arm rests and stretch out. See if you can sleep during the long flight. This little trick of mine actually beats first class!

Oh, by the way, you're not getting my Bud Light!

I've heard about a system called "Martingale" that's used when betting black-jack. Does it work?

The Martingale system is nothing more than doubling your next bet after you've lost, and continue doing so until you win a hand.

This remarkable system works 99 times out of a hundred. But that one time it fails, unfortunately, you will have doubled up your losses to the tune of about $57,856.00 with just enough left in your pocket for a pack of razor blades.

Is there any way a player can control the cards coming out of the shoe?

No. But if you're sitting at a table where a guy zaps the shoe with a blue laser beam coming out of his fingertips, you might want to think the guy's got something going for him.

When I play blackjack, my bets are usually five dollars. Can I get any comps at this level of play?

In most casinos, five dollars will get you a comp for a cup of coffee.

I was watching this guy walk through the casino counting out a bunch of hundred-dollar bills. Isn't this dangerous?

Absolutely. If you're carrying a large wad of bills in the casino, be careful. Never show off your wad in public.

♠ ♠ ♠ ♠

Why do so many dealers act like assholes?

They pick it up from assholes on the other side of the table.

I'm sitting at this blackjack table… it's just me and another guy. He gets all the good cards, pat hands, wins a ton… and me, well, I'm struggling just to stay even. Has this ever happened to you?

It happens to everyone. Here's my advice:

If someone else at the table is winning a lot of money and you're not, it's OK to ask him if he'll trade places with you.

Of course, he'll probably tell you to buzz off, but if he's not sitting on one of the bases, simply get up and move to a spot in front of him. You'll get *his* cards!

I once saw a guy throw both dice off the table and they stuck in this girl's cleavage. And I don't mean just any cleavage. The pit bosses claimed they were the only ones allowed by law to retrieve them. Is this right?

It's one of the few perks of being a pit boss. But I've often wondered what they'd do if the dice landed in some guy's shorts.

When I go to a casino late at night, I always like to take my pit bull with me. Sometimes, you know, I might be walkin' out with a lotta bread on me. Why won't casinos let me take my dog inside? He won't bite anyone unless I tell him to.

A pit bull is not allowed in a casino even if you've trained him to sit at a blackjack table and hold the cards. Pit bosses (not to be confused with pit bulls) are trained to recognize "unusual" players.

Man, I tell ya, everyone in this town is lookin' for a tip. Dealers, waitresses, men's room attendants, change girls, bellhops, I mean everybody! I never give out much in tips but I found that I have to tip the valet guys who bring my car around. When I stiff 'em, they slam the door so hard it knocks the rust off my car!

If you do decide to stiff these guys, make sure you get both legs inside quickly. Las Vegas hospitals are not known for reconstructive surgery.

I live near a casino and I want you to know I've won thousands of dollars thanks to the advice in your books. Unfortunately, I just lost it all in my divorce settlement. Now what?

If you did it once you can do it again. But now, whenever you gamble, always tell your new wife you're just going down to the store.

I'm a professional card-counter and represent a serious threat to any casino's livelihood. I've probably forgotten more stuff about counting than you'll ever learn in a lifetime. That's how good I am. Now I'm at the point where I have to make the bosses think I'm just an average player so they won't pay attention to me. Disguises don't work; I'm over 300 pounds and it's hard to disguise that. What are some things I can say or do when I walk up to a blackjack table that will make the bosses think I'm just some bonehead?

I can give you a list of things, but frankly, I think you're a bonehead anyhow. Try these recommendations and see if they make you any more a bonehead than you already are:

1. Walk up and ask the dealer where the "penny" tables are.

2. If the table's filled with older women, ask the dealer, "How are the old broads doin'?"

3. Throw a bunch of chips on the table and ask the dealer, "Can I use these chips I bought in the gift shop?"

4. Prop your feet up on a chair, take off your shoes and

socks, and pick out the lint between your toes.

5. Spill your drink. Then, spill another one.

6. Ask the dealer if you can see a menu.

7. Tell the dealer you're from Chicago and just in town for a hit.

8. Sit yourself down and open your GI Joe lunch box and take out a banana, a peanut-butter-and-jelly sandwich, and a Twinkie. Tell the dealer, "I only got a half-hour 'cause I gotta get back to school."

9. Dress up like Elvis and keep mumbling, "Thank you very

much, thank you very much." With your weight problem, you'll want to go as the "later" Elvis.

♥ ♥ ♥ ♥

Once when I was playing craps, a player next to me threw up all over the table. Can you believe it?

Hey, I've seen some really ugly dice dealers in my time, but never one so bad that it made me sick… except, now that I think about it… hey, that didn't happen over at the Hilton, did it?

I once saw a guy betting all the spots at a blackjack table for $5,000 a pop. The whole table was reserved for him. Watching him play was really neat. Have you ever seen this before?

Oh sure. These guys are what the casinos call "premium" players. But don't look upon these players as if they're experts or celebrities of some sort. Look upon them for what they really are… idiots.

What can I do to make roulette more exciting to play? I like to play, but frankly, I'm getting bored with it.

You'll be happy to learn that roulette is now the only game in the casino where it is actually legal to use drugs while you play.

The game is so bor-r-r-ing that you'll want to bring along a bottle of No-Doz to keep awake.

And, if you think it's fun to sit there and watch the little white ball go around one way, while the wheel itself turns the opposite way, don't forget to bring your Dramamine. If you get sick in a car, or sick in a plane, you'll get sick at the roulette wheel, too.

You'll also get indigestion when you see your money moving one-way across the table. That's called a "Maalox Moment." So you better bring along a bottle of that, too.

♣ ♣ ♣ ♣

I like to play blackjack where "surrender" is offered. If I don't like my cards, I can surrender the hand and only lose half my bet. Is this a good strategy?

Sure is. And if you surrender all of your bets, you'll cut your losses in half!

I'm a little on the heavy side and have trouble sitting on those little chairs at the blackjack tables. And now the airlines are making me pay for two seats just to fly out there. Isn't this some form of discrimination?

Absolutely. Get a copy of Lenny Shitzelman's book, *Casino Gambling For The Very Obese.* Lenny's advice at the blackjack tables is simple: Just move the chair away and stand at the table. No problem. But the casino might make you play two spots.

I've played keno for several years and never hit a decent ticket. Is there a purpose to this game?

Sure. The casinos love it because the percentages are so steep, and the odds on a nice score are overwhelming.

But the real purpose to this game is in the casinos' restaurants. Keno can keep your kids busy while you busy yourself trying to figure out all the money you've lost. Kids love to play with anything that comes with crayons. And they love to watch the numbers light up on the big keno board.

"Daddy, look at this. All ten of my numbers came up!"

I gamble every weekend. The problem is I'm only 18 years old. If I get caught, will the casino let me keep my winnings?

A better question is will they give you your losses back? You might be surprised to learn that some Indian casinos will actually let 18-year-olds play. And those are usually the casinos situated near a big college. In fancy marketing parlance, that's called "taking advantage of the situation." But seriously, let me give you my stock response to 18-year-olds: Get a job, get an education, and get your hair cut.

I've tried counting the cards at blackjack but it doesn't seem to work for me, even though I've gotten pretty good at it. Is there any other game, like poker or baccarat maybe, where card-counting might also work?

Good question. There are some merits to counting cards at baccarat, but you're still faced with multiple decks. And at the poker tables, every good player knows the importance of keeping track of the cards.

But if you're such a good counter, why not do what my friend does. He counts cocktail waitresses. He assigns a negative value to the ugly ones, and a positive value to the knock-outs. When his count hits +7 he tries to score.

Here's a chart he uses that you can cut out and keep in your wallet:

+2	KNOCK-OUT
+1	NOT BAD
0	AVERAGE
-1	OK IF I'M DRUNK
-2	UGLY
-3	REALLY UGLY

I just bought a good book on blackjack—not yours—and I think I'm ready to play, but I'm a little apprehensive. I'm afraid of making stupid mistakes in front of all the other players. Any advice?

You really don't need my advice. If you make stupid mistakes at the table, the other players will let you know.

It might be something subtle like players rolling their eyes. Or, occasionally, a player will growl when you hit your 16 with the dealer showing a 5. You should also know that it's only a mistake if the dealer makes 20. It's not a mistake, apparently, if your draw makes the dealer bust.

Fascinating game.

♠ ♠ ♠ ♠

I'll never forget the time a blackjack dealer beat me with three 21s in a row. Is there anything I can do to retaliate?

Frankly, I would have walked away after the first two. But, if you really want to get even, I think it's perfectly legal in most casinos to perform the Heimlich maneuver on the dealer's head.

It's amazing how inconsiderate some players are. You should publish a list of table etiquette for gamblers.

Not a bad idea. Here's a list of etiquette based on some of my own observations:

1. If you're a baseball player, do not offend other players by spitting tobacco juice in the ashtray.

2. Do not spill your drink in the dealer's chip-tray. Anywhere else on the table is OK.

3. If you're in town for a medical convention, it is considered rude to ask an attractive blackjack dealer if she wants a free breast exam.

4. Never play blackjack with more than one hat on.

5. Do not walk up to a table in a skimpy swim suit. Unless you're a girl. Then it's probably OK. If I'm at the table, it's definitely OK.

6. If you have managed to accumulate stacks and stacks of chips, do not attempt to build anything with them.

7. Never walk into a casino carrying a violin case.

8. Do not carry your phaser to a blackjack table, unless it's set on "stun."

9. If you're a basketball player, it is not polite to reach up and try to spin the chandeliers.

My business is ball bearings. I sell 'em by the thousands. We got a show we go to in Vegas every year, the big "Machine" show—I'm sure you've heard of it—anyhow, I play a lot of craps when I'm out there and I can tell you something that you probably don't know: Most players don't play often enough to really get good at it. Take me, for instance. Once a year, that's it. It takes me a few hours just to remember everything, like 6s and 8s in multiples of six, you know?

Good point. But you should study up on the game *before*

you get out there. Re-learning the game while you're playing is *not* a good idea. Besides, it's fun to read up on it a week or two before your show. Your preparation at home helps to build up a level of confidence that usually puts you in a positive frame of mind.

But I want to warn you about something: Keep your business and your gambling separate. For example, don't take any of your customers to the dice tables with you. And don't do like one guy I know does when he's out there for a trade show. He passes out his business cards to all the dealers.

Dealers are not interested in ball bearings or hydraulic

pumps. I still don't know why the hell he does that.

And leave your show badge in your room. There's something tacky about walking around a casino with a stick-on badge that says, "HELLO, my name is Al Korwalsky."

Who cares.

Is baccarat a good game to learn?

It's great if you're into snob appeal. Remember, shaken... not stirred.

Sometimes when I'm playing for a long time, I get a severe case of jock-itch and squirm around in my chair. How can I prevent this?

Frankly, I wouldn't worry about it because the other players at the table will just assume you have gas.

♣ ♣ ♣ ♣

What's the advantage of using Basic Strategy at the blackjack tables?

Basic Strategy takes out all the guesswork and gives you at least a mathematically sound explanation as to why you always lose.

My husband and I play blackjack a lot and I'm always afraid he's going to get into trouble because he can be so wild.

Give him a few drinks and there's no telling what he might do.

I know a lot of things are illegal in the casino and would appreciate a list of things that can get players into trouble.

I'll list only those things that I've actually seen happen.

Incidentally, I think I know your husband.

At the blackjack tables, it is against the law to:

1. Hide cards in your mouth.

2. Wear 3-D glasses.

3. Place live animals inside the betting circle.

4. Play footsie with the dealer.

5. Tell the dealer, "Make sure I win 'cause I own the joint."

6. Wear your secret decoder ring.

7. Fly paper airplanes.

8. Win more than three hands in a row.

9. Have sex, even if you're having it alone.

Why do they call the seat at the far right of a blackjack table "first base," and the seat at the far left "third base"?

Think of the table as a football field. The seat at the center of the table is the 50-yard line. Does that help?

I'm becoming a pretty good card-counter. Is there a chance I might be barred from the blackjack tables?

Not if you use a good deodorant.

When should I tip a dealer?

Only when the dealer has been pleasant, helpful, cheerful, courteous, and kind. Since boy scouts and girl scouts are too young to be dealers, I wouldn't worry much about giving out too many tips.

I was sitting at a blackjack table with some of my drinkin' buddies the other night, and the dealer, named Troy, would wink at me every once in a while. Was he trying to help me win?

I doubt it. But just to be safe, I'd get the hell out of there.

I always get to a dice table just about the time some shooter finishes a 20-minute hand.

Same goes for blackjack... I sit down and everyone leaves with their hands cupped full of chips, and I can't win for losin'. What gives?

You remind me of the guy who has a knack for crashing parties just about the time the booze runs out.

The next time I go to the casino, I'm tempted to "bet the farm." Does that make any sense?

It only makes sense if you're tired of walking in cow manure all day, slopping the hogs, and listening to that damn rooster wake you up every morning at 5 a.m.

But here's another option you might consider. Why not sell a half-interest in your farm to the Indians, get a few backers and build a casino right there in the middle of Iowa.

Remember… if you build it, they will come.

I really enjoy playing blackjack, but I've had a lot of problems with dealers. So I'm very careful now about where I sit down. Any recommendations on how to size up a blackjack dealer?

Absolutely. Here's my list of things to look for that might signal a potential problem:

1. Do not play if the dealer talks like Howard Cosell.

2. Be leery of any dealer who spreads the deck and says, "Pick a card, any card."

3. Never play where you see the dealer filing his teeth.

4. Avoid a dealer with a sign around his neck that says, "I play for tips."

5. Stay away from dealers who don't speak English. You won't know when they're cussing you out.

6. Do not play if the dealer looks like Boris Karloff.

7. Pass up the dealer who's always picking lint off the table.

8. Never play with a dealer who claims you remind him of his wife's divorce attorney.

9. Keep walking if you hear the dealer say, "Here's that little twerp again, Lenny."

When I try to strike up a little conversation with a blackjack dealer or just ask a simple question, I find that a lot of them are rude and ignore me all the time. Why would they ignore me like that?

You'll have to excuse me while I go on to the next question.

I always lose. What's my problem?

You're a loser.

Sometimes when I go to the casino, I like to take "Andy" along. But the dealers won't deal to him. They won't even talk to him.

Sometimes, other players will come up and just take his seat away.

My mom calls Andy my "invisible friend," and I guess a casino is just not a good place for him. Right?

I have just the opposite problem. When I'm in a casino on a weekend, I bet I could find a hundred people I would like to *make* invisible.

Is it true, Mr. Shuckelman, that on April the ninth of last year, you lost over two thousand dollars at the Las Vegas Hilton? And isn't it also true, Mr. Shuckelman, that you consistently tell the media that you always win, just to sell books? Isn't that true, Mr. Shuckelman?

What you might be interested in knowing is that I'm able to get casinos to donate 50 percent of my losses to my favorite charities.

In that particular incident, according to my records, a nice donation was made to the Trial Lawyer's Benevolent Fund.

When I play craps, I like to cover all the numbers because I don't want to see some shooter throw a bunch of good numbers that would just go to waste. Anything wrong with this strategy?

Everything is wrong with it! Now listen! What you're doing is what I call "trying to force an opportunity." How do you know a shooter is about to throw "a bunch of good numbers"?

Take my advice and start by betting only a couple of numbers. If you hit 'em, work your way up gradually. But why do I get the feeling I'm giving advice to a fence post?

My name's "Big Mama," and I like to go to the casino in my "Born To Be Wild" T-shirt I picked up at the Harley store. Makes me feel like a man, know what I mean? Just once I want to hear some guy at work tell me to make coffee! I'll knock him on his ass.

So here's my question: How do you feel about swearing at the dice tables? I've found that it's hard to play this game without a little foul language thrown in. You got a problem with that, you stupid f– – –?

Well, I guess it's OK as long as there aren't any women present. I mean, regular women, uh, I mean… feminine women, or, uh, I mean, you know, nice women. Oh, screw it, lady.

I'm a dice dealer, and we got this little Jewish guy who comes in a lot and always irritates the hell out of me. Let me tell you what he does and you tell me how to get rid of this jerk. He questions every payoff over and over again. He doesn't even know what the payoffs should be, but he stops the game all the

time with the same line:
"Scuse me, I was wondering,
is this right? I mean, could
you check this again for
me? I don't think this is
right."

The next time he complains,
check his payoff and say, "By
gosh you're right." Then say
you overpaid him, and take a
few chips away. You'll lose the
jerk in no time.

I'm a little short and have
trouble seeing over the edge
of a dice table. I'm thinking
about asking for a box to
stand on. A dealer asked me

once how Snow White is in bed, and that really pissed me off. Is it OK to drag over a stool from the slot machines to sit on?

Listen, shorty. Don't let people make fun of you just because you're a Munchkin. The next time that dealer smarts off to you, run over to him and punch him in his knees.

My problem is I don't know when to stop. I mean... I can't quit. I just go on and on. Even when I know I should quit, I keep going...

and going. Even people tell me, "Hey buddy, don't you think you should quit now?" But, no, not me, I just keep going. It reminds me of the time when...

I'm sorry I had to cut your question so abruptly but three pages, single-spaced, on both sides of 8-1/2 by 11 paper is a bit much for me. My guess is you probably quit only when you run out of money. So my advice is, leave the ATM card at home.

My psychic told me I should only gamble when the moon is in the Seventh House, and Jupiter aligns with Mars. I don't get it?

This *is* great advice, but only in the fifth dimension. Don't ask me how to get there, but it has something to do with the '60s.

What are the odds of winning on one of those super-jackpot slot machines?

About the same odds of ever hearing these two words used together: "President Quayle."

I just bought my own personal "lucky numbers" from this ad I saw in a magazine. They cost me $39.95. The numbers I got were "1, 2, 3, 4, 5." Do you think I got ripped off?

Yeah. I could have sold them to you for $29.95!

♣ ♣ ♣ ♣

I run an Indian casino up here in Left Overshoe, Minnesota. It gets mighty cold in the winter, and I was wondering if you have any suggestions as to how we can get more customers up

here during these really cold months.

What you need to do is "theme" your casino like all the big Vegas casinos are doing. You can't do Italy and you can't do Paris... the New York skyline is definitely out of the question. Forget mummies and pirates and castles and old Roman stuff. That's been done, too. Everyone's tired of the desert and Old West motifs, so let's look at something really unusual.

I've got it! How about "Siberian Empire." Wow! What an idea! You can reconfigure your casino in the shape of a giant igloo. And inside, all the waitresses can be dressed in short little furry outfits. You can rename your restaurant Nanook's Nook, and serve Cold Duck with frozen TV dinners. Decorations are a snap. Just hang those old plastic, glow-in-the-dark icicles all over the place. To really feel the experience, set your furnace at 40 degrees and bring in some giant fans to simulate howling winds. You'll be raking in cold cash in no time!

I own Lefty's Burger Barn and Casino down here in Mississippi. You folks up North probably don't know about all the casinos we got down here. I'm telling you, everywhere you go, there's a casino sitting on a barge somewhere. Well, the state's after me now for sneaking a few aces out of my blackjack decks, so I'm thinking about packing it up and moving this sucker over to Louisiana. What do you think?

Well, if you want to be competitive over there, you'll have to take all the 10s out of the deck, too!

You probably know my brother-in-law, Benny Noodleman, the famous professional poker player. Well, he's getting up in the years—gotta be 80, I reckon, farts a lot, and he's got these nervous twitches. Really confuses the hell out of the other players. I think this might be good advice for younger players who are too easy to read.

I like it! And this trick might work at the blackjack tables, too, for players who don't like crowded tables.

I just finished reading a new book, *How To Get Rich Playing Roulette*, by Sid Farcus. I can't wait to get started.

It says here in the book that Mr. Farcus owns several yachts, expensive cars, and a big mansion on Long Island. Do you know this guy? Did he really make his money playing roulette?

I think Sid made his money selling books.

I heard that Hyman Zucker still holds the record for drinking the most beers while playing a slot machine. Is this true?

Nope. Hyman lost out in last year's tournament to some young punk who brought in his own Porta-John. You can't imagine the pain Hyman felt. Or maybe you can.

I just cashed in all my slot-club points and all I got was this lousy T-shirt. I spent a lot of money to earn this "prize." Can you believe it?

Let me guess what it says on the shirt: "I just cashed in all my slot-club points and all I got was this lousy T-shirt."

I see you've got a Ph.D. So that makes you a doctor, right?

Right on, baby.
Doctor Shuckelman has a nice ring to it, doesn't it? I'm a psychologist, which means I attempt to explain the reasons behind all the goofy things people do, and no one knows what the hell I'm talking about. The basic premise of psychology is that psychologists aren't

supposed to know what they're talking about. Hey. It works. OK?

♥ ♥ ♥ ♥

A casino I go to advertises that its slot-machine paybacks are 97 percent. They plaster signs all over the place: "Our machines return 97 percent!" Is this good? Why do people fall for this?

Give the casino a buck; it gives you back 97 cents. And players fight each other to play 'em. These people need a psychologist. Oh, I forgot. *I'm* a psychologist. So let's see. Uh, people do this because of, um, uh… the Pythagorean theorem of psychosomatic disorder. Common. Very common.

♣ ♣ ♣ ♣

Our local chapter of the Polish Beer-Tasting Society is having a "Vegas Night" next month, and we want to make sure we don't have the problems we had last time. The cops said we can't do this again unless we've got bouncers at the door. Any other suggestions?

Your problems, obviously, are that too many players are winning! Some people just go berserk when they win a few dollars. Gamblers are a rowdy bunch. You should know that by now. My advice is to either rig the games so they can't win, or force these gambling gluttons to sip a brew or two. That should calm them down.

I think all slot machines are rigged to beat me. Am I right?

Brilliant deduction. Don't tell me you just now figured that out! "Rigged" is a bit strong; let's say "programmed."

Several years ago you published a list of things that gamblers can do to help manage their money. I cut it out and carried it with me in my wallet right there with a picture of my wife, Betty, and my kid—he'll be out in two more years—but some sonofabitch stole my wallet. Any chance you can reprint that list?

Absolutely. It was called "Money Management for Winners," and here it is:

1. Never bet more than you can afford to lose, unless you just don't care anymore.

2. Understand that a wise gambler never loses all his money in one day. It might take two days, three, maybe four.

3. Never play on credit in a casino, unless you have no intention of paying it back.

4. Keep your bets at a safe and sensible level. That way, while other players are winning thousands of dollars, you'll feel good knowing that you won a few bucks, too.

5. Never tip the dealers. These guys make more money than you do!

6. If your chips are dwindling, try to borrow money from

other players at the table. Tell them you're playing for a local orphanage. People will believe anything!

7. While you're playing, tuck away a few chips in your back pocket to ensure that you don't walk away broke. Of course, you'll forget about those chips and they'll just fall out and clog up your washer, but at least they'll be clean.

8. Never gamble when you're tired. If you're half asleep you might forget all the important skills you've acquired and actually win a few bucks.

9.   Don't play in casinos where you usually lose. Of course, I realize this might severely limit your options, so maybe you should just wait for a new one to open.

10. Take frequent breaks while you're gambling. Find the casino's restaurant and order a couple hamburgers. Then back to the tables for a few more hands, followed by a stop at the lounge for a couple beers. Try your luck again, then hit the coffee shop for some strawberry cheesecake. Later on, you can sip a Brandy Alexander poolside. At least this way, you won't be coming home any lighter.

<u>Appendix</u>

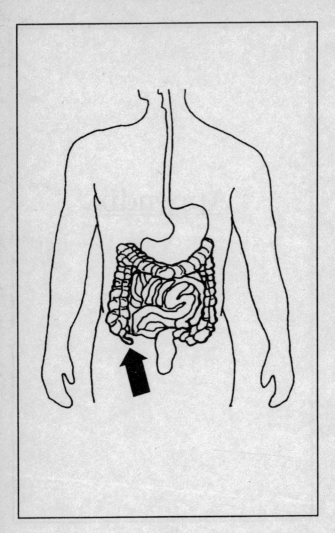

TURN PAGE FOR VALUABLE COUPON!

FREE DRINK!

In The Casino Lounge

Accepted at all U.S., Canadian, and Mongolian casinos!

BUY 5 DRINKS AT THE SPECIAL PRICE OF $3.00
BUY 2 MORE AT THE REGULAR PRICE OF $4.50
GET THE NEXT DRINK FREE!*

*Casino token required. To validate this coupon, check in at the "Promotions" desk between 10 AM and 3 PM weekdays excluding holidays. Take the validated coupon to any "Redemption" booth between the hours of 4 PM and 6 PM and receive your token good for one free drink. Not valid with any other offers. Non-transferrable. Offers may not be combined. Offer limited to quantity on hand. PLEASE NOTE: Retired pro-football linemen are on duty in the lounge to help carry you back to the tables.

TURN PAGE FOR EXCITING OFFER!

Now Available On Video Cassette!

THAT'S RIGHT! *Casino Gambling For Winners* has just been released on video! Order your copy today!

Send only $49.95 plus another $49.95 for shipping and handling (or just send as much money as you can) to:
Box 4, Winnemucca, Nevada 00001.
Allow up to one year for delivery.
Be sure to send only cash. We cannot be responsible for lost checks.

Free Fishing Video!

If you act before midnight tonight, we'll also include a free fishing video, *Fishing For Winners*. You'll hear exciting dialogue like, "Wow, that's a big fish!" and, "Wow, that's a nice fish!" You'll enjoy the moment when these two bumpkins in the boat realize they've actually been catching the same fish over and over again. Which explains why the fish has all these little holes around its mouth. Which begs the question: Is it possible that the fish are in it for the sport, too?

But Wait. There's More!

Order two tapes and we'll throw in our latest release, *Skydiving for Winners*. You'll gasp when you hear the pilot say, "I thought we had *two* engines!!" You'll hold your breath when you hear, "Pull it now." "Pull what?" "The cord!" "Cord? What cord?!" You'll marvel when the cameraman jumps out of the plane with the other guys. Unfortunately, he forgot his parachute, so that part of the tape runs a little short.

For rush delivery, send us the numbers on all your credit cards and we'll pick the one we like.

Publisher's Guarantee

You may return the videos within 30 days if not delighted and take your chances on a refund.